FORT WAYNE IN A NUTSHELL

FORT WAYNE IN A NUTSHELL
a cartoon retrospective

A 20-year anniversary collection of my cartoons
that feature people, places, and things
in my hometown of Fort Wayne, IN.
They were first licensed for publication
by Fort Wayne Magazine,
from the years 2004 to 2017.

Visit Fort Wayne in a Nutshell book on Facebook:
www.facebook.com/profile.php?id=61561919542484

Steve Smeltzer

DEDICATION

To my loving wife, Cynthia ("Cricket"), who patiently waited through 13 years of my morning brainstorming sessions to create sketches that I would submit to Fort Wayne Magazine each month. Then, through the hours it took to ink and color the finished cartoon that would eventually appear in the magazine. And recently, through the months of compiling 75 of these cartoons, formatting, researching, and writing descriptive paragraphs about the subject of the cartoons while learning a new book-designing software. She had to deal with a lot of boring cartoon time. Thanks, Sweetie!

Also, to my family, friends, co-workers, and drum students who have put up with my non-stop, insufferable attempts at humor in just about every situation.

SPECIAL THANKS

Some very kind, inspiring, funny, and creative people have helped me with my cartooning throughout the years. You know who you are, and I'm so grateful to know you. But because of space limitations, I'm only able to thank the following people who had a direct connection to these *Fort Wayne in a Nutshell* cartoons.

Thanks to the incredible team at *Fort Wayne Magazine* starting in 2004, especially Connie Haas Zuber, former editor-in-chief; Beth Heironimus, former senior art director; Caroline Markley, former graphic designer; and Bonnie Blackburn Penhollow, former associate editor/online content editor. Your instrumental role in launching my first cartoons in the magazine cannot be overstated. You were there at the beginning, nurturing a creative and supportive environment that allowed my cartoons to flourish. Your contributions were invaluable, and I am forever grateful.

Thank you, Connie, Beth, Caroline, and Bonnie!

POWERS HAMBURGERS

This cartoon is one of my first cartoons that Fort Wayne Magazine licensed to use as a monthly cartoon feature named "Meanwhile, Back At The Fort." This was in 2004 and would continue to be a monthly feature until 2017. This cartoon is about the character's clothing on the left (looking like John Travolta in Saturday Night Fever) and could be in any setting. So, to make it more relevant to Fort Wayne, I put them in front of a famous local landmark called Powers Hamburgers. Powers has been one of the most popular restaurants in Fort Wayne since 1940!

"My doctor wants to run some tests, but he thinks I've got Saturday Night Fever."

NIGHT OF LIGHTS

This cartoon features an annual event in Fort Wayne called Night of Lights. On the night before Thanksgiving, people come from all over to kick off the season by walking around downtown to watch the lighting of Christmas displays. The event's hallmark is probably Santa's lighting on the north side of the PNC Bank building. This Santa has a long history in Fort Wayne. Starting from 1940 until 1958, this Santa was displayed on the side of the Wolf & Dessauer Department Store building during the Christmas Season.

Timmy Daincourt: Boy Attorney

HEYERLY'S BAKERY

Drive South on Bluffton Road/ Highway 1 for about 12 miles, and you'll see Heyerly's Bakery in Ossian, Indiana. It's on the right and if you can drive past it without stopping for their delicious pastries or doughnuts, you have more willpower than I do.

" No, I love Ossian. I was just imagining something more tropical when you said we'd vacation down South."

GRAND WAYNE CONVENTION CENTER

Around 2005, the renovated and expanded Grand Wayne Convention Center opened in the heart of Fort Wayne. It occupies 225,000 square feet of downtown real estate and is known as the second-largest convention facility in Indiana. When I saw its size and all the windows, I had this idea.

Fortunately, the first convention booked at the new Grand Wayne Convention Center was by The International Window Washers' Union.

WEST CENTRAL NEIGHBORHOOD

The West Central Neighborhood is a residential neighborhood just west of downtown Fort Wayne. It began in the 1830s as a working-class area where the residents could walk to their places of employment. Later, from the 1830s to the 1950s, many prominent families bought properties and built large, beautiful, unique homes. Today, many artists, musicians, actors, writers, and creative people live in West Central and value the rich history and wonderful architecture. Residents take special care when renovating their homes, so I thought, "Hey, why not the dogs?"

"So I thought since it's in West Central,
it would be best to remodel with historical
accuracy."

MASTODONS ON PARADE

In 2005, a city-wide project called Mastodons on Parade was sponsored by Indiana Purdue University Fort Wayne, whose mascot was the mastodon. Around one hundred large fiberglass mastodons were produced, and local businesses and organizations sponsored their own and custom-painted them with a design that was significant to the organization. The finished mastodons were displayed on both sides of Clinton Street by Headwaters Park. I think a circus was in town, at the time that I was thinking of mastodon cartoon ideas and before I knew it, this cartoon was born.

The traveling circus trainers searched all over Fort Wayne for Trunkoo, who had escaped through the element of natural camouflage.

THE HAUNTED CASTLE

Hurricane Katrina hit the United States from August 23 to August 31, 2005. Everyone was talking about what would happen to gas prices if the Gulf refineries were in the path of the storm. A month or so later, this cartoon appeared, highlighting the scary rooms in The Haunted Castle, our local Halloween event.

This year, the scariest room in
The Haunted Castle had to be
The Chamber of Escalating Gas Prices.

PERFECTION SUNBEAM BREAD SIGN

The Perfection Sunbeam Bread sign at 350 Pearl Street has been a fixture among the tops of the buildings in Fort Wayne, Indiana, since 1957. It is equipped with a motor within the sign that makes it appear that the pieces of bread are perpetually falling out of the bread bag. It's an iconic downtown feature installed when the originally named Wayne Biscuit Company became Perfection Bakeries. In the 1990s, they renamed the company to Aunt Millie's Bakeries, a brand of one of their home-style breads that had been very popular. This cartoon shows a possibly nearsighted Paul Bunyan and his love for PB&J sandwiches. Looks like Babe the Blue Ox approves.

Paul made a mental note.
On his way back through Fort Wayne, he needed to bring some peanut butter and jelly.

THE RIVERGREENWAY

The Rivergreenway is a multipurpose trail system winding through Fort Wayne and the surrounding areas. It's remarkable how some of the city's landmarks look so different from the perspective of the trail—almost like you're in a different city. People like to use the Rivergreenway for activities such as walking, biking, running, and, as shown here, dog walking.

Wellington wished his domestic service contract would've had a more detailed description of what it meant to walk the dog on the Rivergreenway.

RURAL ALLEN COUNTY

I don't know why, but I've noticed that some people from rural areas seem to deny that they were raised there. They prefer to appear cosmopolitan, with eclectic and gourmet tastes. You know they grew up on mashed potatoes and gravy, but don't tell anybody. Shhhhh!

"As a matter of fact I was born in a barn.
But, so were you,
'Miss Deny-My-Rural-Allen-County-Roots'."

FORMER McMAHON TIRE LOCATION

This cartoon features the old McMahon Tire building, which eventually became, and still remains, a Starbucks coffee shop. The building stands on the NW corner of Jefferson and Fairfield and has always been a prominent part of Fort Wayne's landscape because of its cool Art Deco design. I believe I drew this cartoon in 2006, around the time construction had begun to turn McMahon Tire into Starbucks. At some point, I was driving by the construction activity and thought how funny it would be if the steeple part of the building would start rumbling, lift off the ground, and rocket into the air.
I probably had too much coffee that day.

In a brief moment of vindication, the frequently doubted, Society of UFO Investigators, watched as the McMahon Tire tower lifted off to join the mothership.

PHILO T FARNSWORTH

An interesting fact about Fort Wayne is that Philo T. Farnsworth, who developed the first all-electronic television system, lived here. The family house still stands close to State Street, near Northside High School. Think of how many things are now possible because of this Fort Wayne inventor.

Timmy didn't share his father's enthusiasm for the newly acquired Farnsworth collectable.

STONER'S FUNSTORE

In the few weeks before Thanksgiving, smart turkeys find a way to fly under the radar. One way is to hide around the farm. Another way is to get a cool disguise. Where are the best costumes or disguises in Fort Wayne? Stoner's on Harrison Street, downtown; that's where. When I was young, I would go down to Stoner's to see the latest magic tricks. You see, Stoner's was, and still is, owned by nationally known magician Dick Stoner. If you were lucky, Mr. Stoner would pick up the magic trick you wanted to buy and perform a brilliant demonstration of it. A world-class magician right in front of you.

Not surprisingly, turkey disguise rentals peaked
in mid-November.

LINCOLN BANK TOWER

This was a fun cartoon to draw for several reasons. First, I thought the idea of Rudolph needing extra money around Christmas and the fact that his "Express Tour" lasted 90 seconds sounded funny. Check out the expressions on his surprised, fast-moving passengers. Another reason this was fun was because my wife and I have always loved the Christmas candles in the windows of the Lincoln Bank Tower The building broke ground two months after the stock market crash of 1929, and construction was finished within a year. Wow, think about that! It was the tallest building in Indiana from 1930 to the early 1970s.

In order to make extra Christmas money, Rudolph took a job with a local carriage company to provide a 90 second express tour of downtown Fort Wayne.

ALLEN COUNTY LIBRARY GENEALOGY CENTER

The Allen County Library in Fort Wayne is the second-largest genealogical library in the United States. People come from all over to learn about their family history and background. It's a very impressive place! This cartoon shows Roger the cat researching the vast amount of information available there to determine that he is related to the cat of Miles Standish, one of the first pilgrims to come over on the Mayflower.

Through the new library's unparalleled Genealogy Center, Roger could prove once and for all, that he was purebred and a direct descendant of the pilgrim, Snowball Standish.

DAYLIGHT SAVING TIME AT THE ALLEN COUNTY COURTHOUSE

Daylight Saving Time. You've got to love it—not!
Boy, I complain endlessly when I need to change the clocks in our house. I can't imagine if I was in charge of changing all the clocks around the city of Fort Wayne—especially this one in the cartoon.

When adjusting the clocks,
Brian preferred to not even think of the phrases,
"spring forward" or "fall back".

THE OLD FORT IN FORT WAYNE, INDIANA

Fort Wayne was named after "Mad Anthony" Wayne, an officer in the Continental Army during the American Revolution. According to the IN.GOV website, Wayne ordered a fort to be built on the shores of the Saint Mary and Saint Joseph rivers in the Miami town of Kekionga. Years later, the current replica at 1201 Spy Run Ave. was built close to the original 1816 location (where the Fort Wayne Fire Department Station #1 sits today). It is so realistic that it would fool even a group of time travelers, as shown here in my 2007 cartoon.

"For the 10th time Henderson, set the time-travel coordinates for Fort Wayne, Indiana, in the year 2007. Clearly, we have arrived hundreds of years early."

Page 17

THE WOMAN IN WHITE

A Fort Wayne legend claims that for many years, a woman in white has been seen walking on Main Street towards the Main Street Bridge (now called Carole Lombard Memorial Bridge). They say The Woman in White walks to the bridge but never reaches the other side. My cartoon theory is that after all this time, many other ghosts from other decades may see her walking there and join her for some fun on a really cool bridge!

Joining the ghost known as "The Lady in White" in this year's halloween haunting of the Main Street Bridge, were "The Lady in Tie-Dye", "The Lady in Denim" and "The Guy in Corporate Casual".

JOHNNY APPLESEED

Johnny Appleseed, born John Chapman, is practically synonymous with Fort Wayne. We have an annual Johnny Appleseed Festival every fall. We have a park named after him, and even our TinCaps baseball team is named in his honor. History says he introduced apple trees to many places, including Pennsylvania, Ohio, and Illinois. However, it was reported that he died here in Fort Wayne. If he had traveled in bare feet, as legend says, the idea depicted in this cartoon would have been a pretty good idea.

If an 18th century Fort Wayne winter was unusually cold, Johnny Appleseed would travel to Florida where he was known as Johnny Orangeseed.

HEADWATERS PARK CHILI FEST

On Sept. 10, 1995, the first phase of Headwaters Park in downtown Fort Wayne opened with a celebration featuring the Foliatum Pavilion sculpture. It had the ability to release clouds of fog into the air. I wasn't there, but the pictures I saw were quite impressive. Several years later, I seem to remember that Headwaters Park hosted a Chili Fest that became an annual event.

Cooking aromas filled Headwater's Park in preparation for all-you-can-eat night at Chili Fest.

THE FESTIVAL OF TREES

I believe the Embassy Theater's Festival of Trees has been a holiday tradition since the 1980s. Its opening night is on the Wednesday evening of The Night of Lights, where all the downtown Christmas lights are lit. People walk through the areas of the Embassy where there are dozens of holiday trees on display. These wonderful trees have been impressively decorated by many businesses and individuals. It really puts you in the spirit, or in the case of this cartoon, it may make you hungry.

"Now remember honey, the number one rule at the Festival of Trees is; All acorns, pine cones and berries are for decorative purposes, only."

GENERAL ELECTRIC SIGN

Younger people may not understand this cartoon because of the scene depicted here. Back when I drew this cartoon, and since the late 1920s, there was a gigantic, iconic sign above the former General Electric building on Broadway Street. It was a big, lighted, circular GE logo with the words General Electric underneath. It was located on the top of the building where the current Electric Works/Do It Best sign is today. Originally, the sign must've used hundreds and hundreds of light bulbs, so I'm sure GE wouldn't have missed one.

It was perfect timing on Christmas Eve,
when Rudolph's nose began to dim,
right above the GE sign.

ARTLINK

Artlink exists to empower artists, encourage creative expression, and enrich Northeast Indiana through engagement in the visual arts. My wife and I know it as a really cool place to visit. Every time we've gone to an art opening, we've always been so impressed with the exhibits and had such a great time with the people we've met there. Check it out. They're located in the Auer Center for Arts and Culture at 300 E Main St, Fort Wayne, IN.

Johnny and Fifi's favorite at Artlink's Fort Wayne Photographer's Exhibit was Rex, whose photos completely captured his subjects' personalities.

THE ICE STORM OF 2008

In December 2008, an ice storm hit Fort Wayne, leaving almost everything covered in ice and thousands of people without power for days. The heavy ice brought down many trees and power lines in our area, requiring extensive cleanup. In a case like this, the best thing to do is hire the experts.

The success of the city's limb pickup project was largely due to the help from expert contractors.

JOHN DILLINGER'S NORTHERN INDIANA HIDEOUT

John Dillinger, born in 1903 in Indianapolis, IN, was an American gangster during the Great Depression. He was the leader of a gang that was accused of robbing many banks in the United States. Dillinger was imprisoned several times and escaped twice. His Midwest crime spree lasted from September 1933 until July 1934. He probably needed to find a place to hide out during that time. Supposedly, the Northern Indiana lake towns were one of them.

Legend has it that John Dillinger and his cronies would often hide out at Webster Lake, trying to blend in with the locals.

FORT WAYNE ROAD CONSTRUCTION

This is a cartoon about wishful thinking. I drew it when road construction was in full swing on the main north-to-south street in downtown Fort Wayne. The building in the background confirms the cartoon's location, which is right across the street from the Allen County Courthouse on South Clinton.

This was definitely a game-changer in Donald's ongoing battle with Fort Wayne's road construction.

SCIENCE CENTRAL

Science Central is an interactive science center in downtown Fort Wayne that is housed in the building of a former utility company called City Light & Power. Around 1987, a group of educational, teaching, business, and engineering leaders developed Science Central to create a discovery center featuring brilliant exhibits and utilizing hands-on participation. It turns out that learning can be fun! Who knew? Bravo, Science Central!

On second thought, combining Science Central's bird watching event with the time machine exhibit, was probably not such a great idea.

PYRAMID BUILDINGS

I'll bet a lot of younger people wonder about these pyramid buildings around the city of Fort Wayne. I think there were originally five of them built in the early 70s for Peoples' Savings and Trust Bank. Prominent architect and designer George Nelson is credited with creating these buildings. In 1972, the building design received the Architectural Award of Excellence from the American Institute of Steel Construction. I don't know what happened to the banks, but some of the buildings still stand and house various successful businesses. The one on Fairfield Avenue was vacant and for sale when I came up with this cartoon around 2009.

No doubt about it. The real estate broker had a good feeling about this potential buyer.

WOLF & DESSAUER CHRISTMAS SHOW WINDOW

You can ask practically any Fort Wayne Baby Boomer about their childhood memories of the W&D's show windows at Christmas time, and you'll probably hear a story. Wolf and Dessauer (W&D) was a large multi-level department store, much like the stores depicted in movies like *Miracle on 34th Street* or *Elf*. Each year, around Thanksgiving, W&D would display a wonderfully stocked and decorated toy department that was beyond words to most children. But, before you even got inside, you would see that the retail show windows were now devoted to animatronic elves, busy in Santa's workshop, as well as children, cute animals, toys, trains, reindeer, and all things Christmas, moving around in a magical, snowy Christmas landscape.

"Unless you have three hours to kill, I wouldn't ask Grandma and Grandpa about something called the W&D's Christmas window."

MAD ANTS VS THE KOMETS AT THE COLISEUM

That would be a crazy game between Fort Wayne's two professional sports teams. Of course, it couldn't happen now. The Fort Wayne Komets still play at the Coliseum and have a tremendous amount of loyal fans. However, the Mad Ants basketball team, affiliated with the Indiana Pacers, left Fort Wayne and is now based in Indianapolis. I was never too fond of the name Mad Ants. "Ants" sounds so diminutive, not powerful, as many sports teams' names do. Of course, the name Mad Ants was based on Mad Anthony Wayne, who our city was named after, but how do they explain the name down in Indy?

A scheduling blunder at the Allen County War Memorial Coliseum made for a very interesting game between the Mad Ants and the Komets.

ABOITE BIKE TRAILS

I seem to remember that I drew this cartoon when the Fort Wayne bike trail system was finishing up completion on the Aboite bike trails. It was built to connect with some of the city's older bike trails. Currently, the entire trail network consists of more than 120 miles of trails in the Fort. These trails provide benefits for recreation and fitness and are just a way for people to get back and forth to jobs, events, or whatever. The trails see over 60,000 people a month during the summer. More if you count the people on the old trails who have been wandering around since 1870.

The Aboite bike trails were designed to connect to some of the city's older bike trails.

FORT WAYNE FESTIVALS

During the summer months in Fort Wayne, it's one festival after another at Headwaters Park. About every weekend from the end of April to the end of September, you can drive down South Clinton Street and see crowds of people walking towards the sights and sounds of celebration in the pavilion at the park. It's easy to see how our cartoon family below could get mixed up.

The gyros, the baklava, the circle dancing. It slowly dawned on the Oopsenheimer family that this was not Germanfest. This was Greekfest.

JUNK FOOD ALLEY

The Three Rivers Festival started in 1969 as a community celebration on The Landing along Columbia Street. It has developed into the second-largest summer festival in Indiana. One of the big features is Junk Food Alley, and it will not disappoint. There's always something for everyone: BBQ, Sirloin Tips, Ice Cream, French Fries, Slushies, Lemon Shake Ups, Chicken on a Stick, Carmel Corn, Funnel Cakes, and yes, You-know-what-Ears.

"If you can get past the name,
they really are quite delicious."

FOELLINGER THEATRE

Adjacent to the Fort Wayne Children's Zoo in Franke Park stands the Foellinger Theatre. This open-air, covered theater has been in this location since 1941. Throughout the years, it has been host to a myriad of entertainment events, such as national music acts, orchestral concerts, plays, and even free summer movie nights. It is wonderful all-ages entertainment. By the looks of this cartoon, possibly all species, too.

Where The Wild Things Are was definitely one of the favorite movies of the locals who attended the Foellinger Theatre Summer Movie Series.

WELLS STREET CORRIDOR

Because of a collaboration between the city of Fort Wayne and the Wells Area Merchants, a new streetscape plan was implemented in the Wells Street Corridor. As I remember, it was around 2010 that these businesses invested in new building facades to enhance the area's beauty. The city and the neighborhood, together, introduced new brick paver sidewalk inserts, benches, bike racks, and these things called bollards. The bollards are short posts delineating a line between pedestrians and motor traffic.

Area dogs applauded the renovations.

"If you're like me, your mind goes right to fire hydrants, doesn't it?"

SWEETWATER

What started as founder Chuck Surack's Volkswagen bus recording studio has become a billion-dollar music technology and musical instrument retailer called Sweetwater. I saw it first-hand as he had transitioned the studio into his home and eventually continued to expand into subsequent larger locations. Each location added more products and services while hiring more employees. The current location is a sprawling campus with a retail store, recording studios, auditorium, outdoor music pavilion, music lesson academy, shipping facility, repair center, and sales and marketing offices. But that's not all. There are arcade games, open mic stages, a salon, a coffee bar, a full-service restaurant, and an expansive dining area! You really need to see it to believe it! Sweetwater is located on the corner of US Hwy 30 W & Kroemer Road.

"I had a blast at Sweetwater, playing arcade games, joining a drum circle, eating in their diner, getting a latte at the coffee bar, and listening to a jazz jam session. But I got halfway home before I remembered that I had gone there to buy a guitar."

STARBUCKS IN DOWNTOWN FORT WAYNE

The Starbucks gift card is a perfect go-to present for just about anybody on your Christmas list. The coffee company designs the cards with the particular season in mind. They always look so festive and are available at prices that fit anyone's budget. Lonnie the Bear, shown in this cartoon, values his Starbucks gift cards so much that he has prioritized coffee over nature.

"Hibernate-shmibernate", said Lonnie the Bear, as he used up another one of the 15 gift cards that he got for Christmas.

CAPTAIN HOOK AT THE BOTANICAL CONSERVATORY

The Foellinger-Freimann Botanical Conservatory, a part of the Fort Wayne Parks and Recreation Department, is a large public space in downtown Fort Wayne that features three different garden rooms of plants from all over the world. In addition to the plants, the Botanical Conservatory hosts many events and exhibits throughout the year. In January of 2011, a Peter Pan exhibit opened for a three-month run. It featured representations of famous settings from the original stage play, including the Lost Boys' Camp and, of course, the Pirates' ship. Some kids arrived dressed as different Peter Pan characters and enjoyed interacting with the displays. This cartoon shows Captain Hook working overtime.

To make ends meet, Captain Hook volunteered for other jobs around the Botanical Conservatory, besides the Peter Pan exhibit.

FOSTER PARK GOLF COURSE

In 1928, Fort Wayne's first public golf course opened in Foster Park on Old Mill Road. This was largely made possible by the generous donation of 110 acres of land by Samuel and David Foster in 1912. Imagine: this golf course has been in existence for almost 100 years. If this cartoon was drawn in the 1920s, do you suppose the wife would've been dropping the husband off in a horse and carriage?

"Thanks, honey. I'll see you in November."

MORE FORT WAYNE FESTIVALS

It seems like Fort Wayne has a different festival every week each summer, and most festivals go on for multiple days. Arab Fest, Germanfest, BBQ RibFest, GreekFest, Three Rivers Festival, Pride Fest, Fiesta Fort Wayne, and Taste of the Arts are some of the popular ones that occur around Headwaters Park. If you went to all of them, you'd probably look like the woman in this cartoon.

"The exhaustion and the multiple wristbands in the month of June, all point to a diagnosis of Fort Wayne Fest Fatigue."

HUMIDITY IN FORT WAYNE

I often joke with my friends in Fort Wayne that I'm in a constant state of sweating from the first of May to the end of October. But, as Mark Twain said about New England's weather, we also say about Fort Wayne, "If you don't like the weather in Fort Wayne now, just wait a few minutes."

"Even by Fort Wayne standards,
this is a very humid July!"

THE ARTS UNITED CENTER

Do you ever see faces in inanimate objects? I think that many times, certain cars take on a personality because of the design of the front grill and headlights. I know my 1969 Volkswagen Beetle was like that. Well, for some reason, The Arts United Center (originally called the Theatre of Performing Arts) on Main Street, next to the Art Museum, was like that to me. I always saw a jack-o'-lantern. Anybody else?

Frankly, the Arts United Center has always been just a coat of paint and a couple of candles away from being a very cool jack-o'-lantern.

FORT WAYNE PARKING CONTROL DEPARTMENT

I've never lived anywhere except Fort Wayne, so I don't know if parking control departments in other cities are like ours, but boy, does the Fort Wayne Parking Control Department take their jobs seriously. And with extreme promptness! There, that's a nice way of saying it, isn't it? Santa finds this out in this cartoon, and as a result, he may just be adding a new name to the Naughty List.

Sure, he was "a little old driver, so lively and quick", but still he was no match for the Fort Wayne Parking Control Department.

CITY GLASS SPECIALTY, INC.

City Glass Specialty, Inc. was established in 1944. Originally, it was meant to be a stained glass business serving the needs of churches in the area. Shortly thereafter, the residential, automotive, and commercial departments developed to add to the already established stained glass business. Through 80 years of serving the Fort Wayne area, they've become one of the most well-known and trusted companies, specializing in all kinds of glass needs and repairs for homes and businesses. Because my wife and I renovated our 100-year-old house with a bazillion 5" window panes, I've spent many days at City Glass. In my opinion, they are unsurpassed in expertise and hometown friendliness.

"It's a beautiful window installation.
Now, let's roll it down and give it a test drive."

3 RIVERS CO-OP NATURAL GROCERY

The 3 Rivers Co-op Natural Food & Deli is a full-line natural grocer that offers bulk foods, fresh organic produce, frozen and refrigerated goods, and a large selection of natural grocery products. They also feature an eat-in deli and café serving homemade foods from an onsite kitchen. They began in the 70s as a natural food-buying club with members who would order, receive, and distribute food to themselves. Now, they are in a much bigger place and open to the public. I go there about twice a week and love the food and the people who work there! Although I've never seen any chickens walking around the parking lot, I can see how the name may confuse them.

"I told you it was pronounced 'co-op'
and not 'coop'".

ZESTO ICE CREAM

Zesto, the iconic ice cream stand, has been on the corner of Creighton and Broadway in Fort Wayne for over fifty years. Our family would go there in the 1960s because our grandparents lived about a block away. Talk about being in the right place at the right time! Soft-serve ice cream, in the summertime, within walking distance. We still go there, and it looks and tastes pretty much the same. Delicious!

"First of all, I'd like to thank my grandparents for their generous support in my extensive research of the historic Broadway corridor landmark known as Zesto."

SUMMIT CITY COMIC CON

As I remember, Fort Wayne (also known as the Summit City) and the Grand Wayne Center really had a comic con convention for a few years, but it didn't continue for long. Too bad, because I think it's always cool to be driving downtown and seeing business people and superheroes walking side by side. Plus, the presence of Superman, Batman, or Professor Whirlybird just may be a very effective crime deterrent.

Superhero enthusiasts from all over the country traveled to the 2012 Summit City Comic Con. Some, like Professor Whirlybird, saved dramatically on travel expenses.

EDY'S AND DREYER'S ICE CREAM

When I drew this cartoon in the early 2010s, this building at 3426 North Wells Street had the Edy's sign displayed on the outside brick wall. Now, the name Dreyer is also prominently shown. I wondered what was happening recently, so I did a little research. In 1928, ice cream maker William Dreyer and candy maker Joseph Edy formed a partnership and created Dreyer's and Edy's Ice Cream. Eventually, the ice cream was sold all over the U.S., with Dreyer's Grand Ice Cream being marketed in the west and Edy's Ice Cream being marketed in the east. A rose (or ice cream cone) by any other name would smell (or taste) as sweet.

"Look over to your right, honey and you'll see where Mommy does some of her best work."

THE JOHNNY APPLESEED FESTIVAL

The Johnny Appleseed Festival, one of the biggest festivals in Fort Wayne, happens in Johnny Appleseed Park on the third full weekend in September every year. It began in 1974 with about 20 vendors and now has grown to an impressive count of approximately 200 food, artisan, demonstration booths, entertainment stages, and playground areas. All participants and their booths are required to have the look of the 1800s. Even the food must be cooked over a fire to ensure historical authenticity. It's a wonderful festival in a beautiful setting at a perfect time of the year. There's nothing like walking on crunchy leaves and smelling the fires that make delicious home-cooked food. Finally, even though there are thousands of people there, it seems like we always run into a lot of friends. Like our friends, the bees are talking about it below. They seem to really like it there, too.

"I've got an idea.
Let's get six thousand friends together
and go out to the Johnny Appleseed Festival
this weekend."

GLENBROOK DODGE FLAG

I drew this cartoon back when the Giant American Flag flew proudly above the Glenbrook Dodge car dealership on West Coliseum Blvd. The flag was raised on October 13, 2001, to celebrate the dealership's 20th anniversary. It was known as one of the largest continuously flying flags in the U.S. Glenbrook Dodge continued to fly it out of appreciation for their country, community, and customers throughout the years. According to their website, the original flag was made of 80 pounds of nylon and measured 50 feet by 80 feet. It flew 232 feet in the air. The flagpole was 43 inches in diameter. The pole weighed 35,600 pounds, and the base contained 400,000 pounds of concrete. Unfortunately, on December 23, 2022, with wind chills reaching -38°, the flag pole snapped into three pieces. As a result, the flag pole needed to be re-evaluated and re-engineered for a possible upcoming encore. UPDATE: Good news! We saw them installing the new flagpole on June 28, 2024, days before this book's publication.

Rudolph had calculated the height for an average flag. But obviously, the flag at Glenbrook Dodge was not an average flag.

THE FORT WAYNE KOMETS

Early in the 1950s, a man named Ernie Berg had heard that Fort Wayne was planning to build the Allen County War Memorial Coliseum. He became very excited as he thought of the possibility that the Coliseum could be an ideal place to host hockey games. After he went to Toledo one night to watch an IHL game, Berg returned and started working on this dream. The dream became a reality when the first game was played at the beginning of the 1952-1953 International Hockey League season. Throughout the years, the Fort Wayne Komets have received ten championship titles. They remain extremely popular, are exciting to watch, and bring in thousands of loyal fans.

"In my defense, it looks a lot like a hamburger from up here in the stands."

SWINNEY PARK TENNIS COURTS

Colonel Thomas W. Swinney's last will and testament decreed that the land on which his 1844-built house stood would be given to the city of Fort Wayne after the last of his three beneficiary daughters had died. In 1893, the city decided to lease the land from the Swinney daughters. In 1923, the last surviving daughter passed away, and the city took possession of the land. From 1920 to 1940, a man named George F. Trier leased the park and opened an amusement park called Trier Park. In 1953, it was turned back into a typical park and is now known as East Swinney and West Swinney Parks. West Swinney is notable for ball diamonds, a Japanese pavilion, natural open spaces, an 18-hole disc golf course, and a basketball court. East Swinney is recognized for its fishing area, natural open spaces, the Rivergreenway, the Swinney Homestead, and, as shown below, tennis courts.

In The Trees Around Sweeney Park's Tennis Courts

LAKE WAWASEE FIREWORKS

Northeastern Indiana loves two things in particular: lakes and fireworks. Put the two together, and you have an extravaganza. Such an extravaganza happens annually at the beginning of July at Lake Wawasee in Syracuse, Indiana. Residents, friends, and family in the Lake Community line up on the shore or jump in boats to watch this spectacular event. It usually seems to be scheduled on a date other than July 4th. Maybe that's to make it convenient for people who want to see their hometown's fireworks and those at Wawasee. Nevertheless, this occasion will surely bring out the patriotism in people and fish alike.

It took something especially patriotic, like the Wawasee fireworks, to bring out the rarely seen Red, White and Bluegills.

LAKE JAMES

Speaking of lakes, Lake James is the 4th-biggest lake in Indiana. It is a glacial lake and is home to Pokagon State Park, named in honor of two Potawatomi leaders: Simon Pokagon and his father, Leopold. Lake James is known for boating, fishing, and recreation. This cartoon is set on the lake, in front of the hotel and restaurant called the Potawatomi Inn. My wife and I try to go there every year, before the 4th of July, to listen to The Patriotic Pops concert performed by The Fort Wayne Philharmonic. They set up on the shoreline, facing the Potawatomi Inn, while people sit in lawn chairs and listen from the grassy area between the inn and the lake. Also, boat owners travel up close to the shore to listen from the water.

"Dad, I think we know Lake James well enough, to call it Lake Jim."

DeBRAND FINE CHOCOLATES

DeBrand Fine Chocolates' owner, Cathy Brand-Beere, started making candy in her family's Fort Wayne home at the age of 8 years old. Years later, in 1987, she started the internationally known DeBrand Fine Chocolates. The following year, she married Tim Beere, and they continue working together in the company. The DeBrand name comes from the French "De," which means "from" and Cathy's last name, "Brand." Initially, the first store was located in her childhood home and has now expanded to two retail shops in Fort Wayne and one in Indianapolis. The company employs nearly 100 people, and their candy is available nationwide in retail stores. They also have a department that ships DeBrand Fine Chocolates worldwide. This cartoon shows that even though trick-or-treating is a numbers game and kids try to visit as many houses as possible, a few treats are definitely worth the extra effort. If you've tasted DeBrand truffles, you know what I mean.

"Yes, it's a long walk to the door.
Yes, they're probably closed.
But that's a risk I'm willing to take."

MAYOR TOM HENRY

Tom Henry, the thirty-fifth mayor of Fort Wayne, held the office from January 2008 until March 2024, serving the longest of any Fort Wayne mayor. He was elected to five terms, serving an impressive sixteen years in office. He was known to many as "The People's Mayor". Under his watch, Fort Wayne experienced some fantastic changes, such as the building of Parkview Field, the development of the Dr. Martin Luther King Jr. Memorial Bridge, a riverfront project that brought to the downtown area a place known as Promenade Park, and most recently, the redevelopment of the old General Electric building into a mixed-use place known as Electric Works. I used to joke with my friends about Downtown Fort Wayne becoming a ghost town. All that seemed to be down there were a few restaurants and lawyer offices. Now, because of Mayor Henry's influence, Downtown is vibrant again. Sadly, Mayor Henry passed away on March 28, 2024. Almost unbelievably, he died about two months after Cindy, his wife of forty-nine years, passed away. The cartoon below was published in Fort Wayne Magazine around 2013, and I always wondered if he saw it.

"Hold it, Buddy! I've got Mayor Tom Henry on the phone, and he's given me a full pardon!"

SCIENCE CENTRAL'S SMOKESTACKS

The Science Central Building at 1950 North Clinton Street originally housed City Light and Power, the first publicly-run electric utility built in 1908. It utilized coal-powered steam generators and three boilers, so it's pretty obvious why there are gigantic smokestacks on top of the building. Science Central was originally incorporated as a non-profit organization in 1987. Then on November 5, 1995, they opened their doors and the minds of Fort Wayne residents to a wide world of scientific discovery. At some point, they painted the multiple smokestacks in a multi-colored theme, which is easier for Santa to see from the air but doesn't necessarily help him choose the correct one for gift delivery.

"Do you remember which chimney we use here at Science Central?"

FOELLINGER-FREIMANN BOTANICAL CONSERVATORY

I have a friend who likes golfing because he says that it feels really good just to look around at all that green. I think for many people, it's the same with the Foellinger-Freimann Botanical Conservatory. Right there, in the middle of downtown Fort Wayne, we find an oasis of living green things within the walls of the conservatory's three garden rooms. First is the Showcase Garden, which includes beautiful seasonal displays and exhibits. Another room, The Tropical Garden, is devoted to rainforest-type plants around a cascading waterfall. Finally is the Desert Garden, which displays cacti and other beautiful plants like you would find in places, mostly out West. Obviously, the plants at the Foellinger-Freimann Botanical Conservatory are beautiful, but please, they're not supposed to be delicious.

"We were thinking it was the world's greatest salad bar until we were kicked out of what turned out to be the Botanical Conservatory."

THE FORT WAYNE CHILDREN'S ZOO

The Fort Wayne Children's Zoo started as a nature preserve in Franke Park. The year was 1952, and the preserve was home to some not-so-exotic animals. A black bear, some monkeys, wildcats, deer, mountain goats, an American Eagle, and other animals you could find if you drove a few miles out of town to a wooded area. The preserve became popular, and by 1962, work began to build a zoo. A few years later, on July 3, 1965, the Fort Wayne Children's Zoo opened on its first day to 6000 people. Throughout the years, the zoo has added numerous areas, including the African Journey, the Australian Adventure, and most recently, the Asian Trek areas. By the way, I think the girl in this cartoon really took a shine to the area called Monkey Island.

"Wait. How many kids did we have when we came in here?"

DOWNTOWN FORT WAYNE CONDOMINIUMS

It seems like around the mid-2010s, every downtown Fort Wayne street that you drove down had a condominium or apartment project underway. I think this was mainly because of Mayor Tom Henry's downtown revitalization projects. The theory was probably to bring in new restaurants, shops, festivals, and entertainment venues so it would cause people to want to live in the middle of it. It looks like it worked. I specifically remember when I first started seeing many young adults riding their bicycles around downtown Fort Wayne in the evening. It was kind of a strange sight compared to the scarce pedestrian traffic I was used to seeing in downtown after 5 pm. All I know is that Fluffy, in the cartoon below, is very proud to reign over this jewel of Northeast Indiana.

Tiffany and Fluffy's first day in their new condo.

I&M PEREGRINE FALCON WEBCAM

In the early 1990s, the Indiana Department of Natural Resources (IDNR) built a cozy Peregrine Falcon nesting box high atop the Indiana Michigan Power Center building in downtown Fort Wayne. Since then, several falcon families have made their homes high up there to hatch and raise their chicks (called "eyases"). Every year, people can watch the nesting families of this raptor species on a webcam. The IDNR and volunteers from Soarin' Hawk Rescue and the Indiana Audubon Society care for the birds by providing medical care, cleaning up the nest, and tracking their locations. I remember when these nesting boxes were installed. It was supposed to attract falcons to the area, which, in turn, would help to control the increasing pigeon population naturally. Pigeon droppings can create health and safety issues. Since pigeons instinctively know to avoid falcons, Fort Wayne stays cleaner and safer with the presence of families, as illustrated in the cartoon below. Side note: I drew this cartoon in the mid-2010s before I&M changed from their old logo (pictured) to their new one.

"Your dad is acting like a celebrity because
he just realized the I&M FalconCam
is watching us."

OLD FORT EVENTS AND TOURS

I learned while writing this cartoon's paragraph that, throughout the years, there were five forts built within a square mile of the center of what we now call Downtown Fort Wayne. The earliest fort was built by the French in 1722 and was located near the intersection of VanBuren and Superior. The first U.S. fort was completed in 1794 and was located where Clay and Berry Streets meet today. Today's Old Fort at 1201 Spy Run Ave is a replica of the last Fort that stood here in 1816. These forts have a complicated and fascinating history involving the Iroquois, British, French, and original tribes, including the Miami tribe that formed a village at the confluence of the three rivers called Kekionga. You can learn more about The Old Fort online or by visiting the grounds during operating hours. Just don't tell the kids that they'll probably learn something.

"I'll go to The Old Fort with you, but remember that it's still summer vacation, so don't try to teach me any history."

CHARLIE BROWN TREE AT THE FESTIVAL OF TREES

A Charlie Brown Christmas. This wonderful animated special, written by *Peanuts* comic strip creator Charles Schulz, made its CBS television network debut on December 9, 1965, and ran each year until 2000. ABC bought the broadcast rights and began running the special annually from 2001 until the last broadcast on December 17, 2019. In October 2020, Apple TV+ acquired exclusive rights to all *Peanuts* specials and offered them only on their streaming service. The fact that *A Charlie Brown Christmas* and the other *Peanuts* specials were no longer on network television caused such a public outcry that AppleTV+ decided to allow PBS to run the special in 2020 and 2021. Those were the last times the special aired on network TV, ending a 57-year run. I'm so sad that many young people will never see this wonderful special on TV unless they subscribe to AppleTV+. I know, I know, there are always DVDs, but it's not the same for me. The scrawny tree in the cartoon below was in the special's last scene and helped to depict the true meaning of Christmas. I thought it would be funny to imagine the characters in the special coming to The Festival of Trees and decorating this tree so it became majestic, like in the TV special.

A late entry in the Embassy's Festival of Trees.

ALLEN COUNTY CHRISTMAS TREE RECYCLING PROGRAM

In Fort Wayne, it's a win-win-win situation for live Christmas tree owners, Christmas tree recycling centers, and the little guys in the cartoon below. Many people like having a live tree for Christmas, but one of the hassles is, what do you do with it after the holiday has ended? Fortunately, Fort Wayne has a great Christmas tree recycling program. The Allen County Department of Environmental Management offers free Christmas tree recycling at various drop-off sites around Fort Wayne and surrounding Allen County. Simply take your tree to one of the designated areas within the hours they will accept drop-offs, and they will be turned into mulch for use by county parks and local organizations. That is unless the little guys in the cartoon don't get to the trees first. In that case, bon appétit!

"Same time, same place, every year, the kind people of Fort Wayne drop off these delicious trees for us to enjoy."

THE REVITALIZATION OF DOWNTOWN FORT WAYNE

When I drew this cartoon in 2015, there was a lot of talk about how Downtown Fort Wayne was changing. The Grand Wayne Convention Center had already expanded to 225,000 square feet, the Harrison Square project was underway, Parkview Field was open, the revitalization of the Landing was expected to be completed in four or five years, Promenade Park would open in 2019, Union Street Market in Electric Works would open in November 2022, and new restaurants and retail spaces were appearing everywhere. All these options were wonderful for the go-getters, but although I enjoy these opportunities, sometimes I find it nearly impossible to escape the gravitational pull of the couch.

"I would like to sue the City of Fort Wayne for becoming more and more vibrant, which is disrupting my couch potato lifestyle."

POWERS HAMBURGERS AND CONEY ISLAND

At the heart of this cartoon are two legendary Fort Wayne restaurants known for bringing friends, families, and strangers together in a wonderful bouquet of onion smells. The two restaurants are, of course, Powers Hamburgers and Fort Wayne's Famous Coney Island Wiener Stand, founded in 1940 and 1914, respectively. If you haven't eaten at these restaurants, you're seriously missing out. I have a college music professor friend who visited Fort Wayne years ago to play some gigs with a band I played drums in. The band introduced him to one of these restaurants, which he loved. He loved it so much that years later, I got a call from him while he was traveling with some students from the Midwest to the East Coast. They were passing through northern Indiana, and he called to get directions because he had told his students about the delicious lunch he had experienced years before. I gave him directions, and he promptly detoured to Fort Wayne to let his students taste it for themselves. People love these two restaurants and, ipso facto, the smell of onions.

"And this is our hermetically sealed break room for employees who choose to bring back food from Powers or Coney Island."

AUNT MILLIE'S BAKERY

What is better than the wonderful smell of baking bread? That familiar aroma can stir up happy memories of family, warm kitchens, and simpler times. Some might not know this, but there was a time when most of downtown Fort Wayne had a wonderful smell of baking bread in the air. You see, there used to be a large bread bakery on Pearl Street called Aunt Millie's, and what a glorious smell emanated from that building! Although their bread is still available in area stores, unfortunately, we don't get to smell it baking. They made the decision to close the Pearl Street location on April 12, 2018. The closure was because some grocery stores had closed, and they only needed six of their seven bakeries. Aunt Millie's headquarters still remain in Fort Wayne.

"Set the coordinates for Downtown Fort Wayne, or just stick your head out the window and let me know when you smell bread baking."

ABOITE TOWNSHIP

Aboite is a township in Allen County that has become a desirable residential area. Population figures list Aboite's population in 1990 as 18,492 people. Fast forward to 2022, and the estimated population was 42,783 people. As you can imagine, parks, shopping centers, and restaurants appeared as more houses were built. Families moved in, and schools materialized. I think I drew this cartoon in the middle of this residential boom. I included this cartoon in this book for two reasons. First, I like to use anthropomorphic characters in cartoons. The second reason is that the cartoon uses the classic my-dog-ate-my-homework cliché, a humorous excuse that a student used because the student's homework was not done. Now that laptops are used for most school work, even the memory of handwritten homework will soon be a thing of the past.

"The great thing about Aboite is that it's very close to many schools, so there's always plenty of homework to eat."

BROADWAY SHOWS AT
THE HISTORIC EMBASSY THEATRE

The Historic Embassy Theatre, the Crown Jewel of
Fort Wayne's performance arts, was built in 1928. Its long history and
beautiful architecture are so important that it was placed on the
National Registry of Historic Places in 1975. The Embassy Theatre
features national concert acts, films, and many plays from Broadway.
When I drew this cartoon in 2016, such a Broadway production was
slated to appear at the Embassy. The production was *Annie*, and I
thought about the famous song that Annie sang and tied it to the
sentiment of the ever-changing Fort Wayne weather. Actually, I
imagine many other cities complain about their own fickle weather.

At the rehearsal
for the Embassy's production of *Annie*.

"MAD ANTHONY" WAYNE

I heard that a gentleman from Fort Wayne was on an airplane and struck up a conversation with the person sitting next to him. When the gentleman said he was from Fort Wayne, the other passenger assumed he was from a United States Army post, like the places where recruits go to complete Basic Training Boot Camp. Fort Wayne was actually named after General Anthony Wayne, an American Revolutionary War general who oversaw the building and completion of Fort Wayne in 1794. He got the nickname "Mad Anthony" Wayne, not because of his battlefield behavior but because of a misbehaving soldier whom New Jersey law officers arrested. The soldier demanded that General Wayne be contacted to help him, but instead of helping him, Wayne threatened to have him flogged. The soldier was reported to have said, "Anthony is mad!"

The name Mad Anthony was just a military persona. His friends actually knew him as Reasonable Tony.

TINCAPS BASEBALL TEAM

Speaking of funny, I thought, well into my adulthood, that the phrase "for all intents and purposes" was "for all intensive purposes." And don't get me started on how I thought the word "hyperbole" was pronounced, "high-per-bowl." So, I can understand that this cat, in his cat world of cat food, cat toys, and cat naps, could naturally think that the TinCaps, Fort Wayne's High-A Minor League Baseball team, was really named the TinCats. Speaking of the TinCaps, they got their name as a salute to historical legend Johnny Appleseed, who had ties to Fort Wayne and reportedly wore a metal pot for a hat. The TinCaps play their home games at the outstanding Parkview Field, which has been recognized as the country's No. 1 Minor League Baseball ballpark experience. They are affiliated with the San Diego Padres of Major League Baseball.

"Wanna hear something funny? All this time,
I thought their name was the TinCats."

FORT WAYNE RIVERFRONT DEVELOPMENT

This cartoon was drawn when the city's excitement about the proposed Riverfront Development was at a high point. A lot was going on regarding the designing, funding, and legal issues involved with the project. So much positive momentum and excitement in the city was being experienced about all the new ideas. Ideas that included a beautiful park with a park pavilion, event lawn, entry plaza with sculpture, educational water features, urban streetscape, central plaza, urban riverfront terraces, elevated boardwalk, dock, river boating activities, and children's play area. About three years later, on August 9, 2019, Promenade Park opened to rave reviews! I think it exceeded many people's expectations. I think it was perfect timing for this cartoon family from Black Lagoon, Arkansas, who were planning to relocate to Fort Wayne for more employment opportunities.

"...And here's the best reason to move to Fort Wayne. They're planning a really cool riverfront development!"

NPR WBOI 89.1 FM

Fort Wayne has a wonderful National Public Radio Member Station called WBOI. It is located at 89.1 on the FM dial and is owned and operated by Northeast Indiana Public Radio, a non-profit organization. WBOI offers a vast array of national and local radio programming. National radio shows such as *Morning Edition, Here & Now, All Things Considered,* and the tremendously popular *Fresh Air*, hosted by the American journalist Terry Gross. A few popular local programs include shows like *WBOI Presents, The Burnt Toast Show*, and *Tossed Jazz Salad*. In addition, two very important local radio shows are *Folktales* and *Meet The Music*, which are both hosted by the VIP of our local broadcasting arts and culture scene, Julia Meek. The girl in the cartoon is very lucky to have a mom who is "tuned in.".

"The kids at school talk about women named Rihanna and Taylor Swift. But, because of your WBOI obsession, the only names I know are Terry Gross and Julia Meek."

BERNE SWISS DAYS

Every year, Berne, IN, hosts a celebration on the last Thursday, Friday, and Saturday of July. What started 50 years ago as a sidewalk sale for downtown businesses and was called Berne Summer Days has evolved into the well-known Berne Swiss Days. People (including my wife and I) come from all over to take part in this small-town, almost Mayberry-like, three-day festival celebrating Berne's Swiss heritage.

The town closes down the main streets to make room for merchandise, food, and craft vendors, in addition to a tent where the sound of polka music and dancing adds an authentic Swiss soundtrack to the fun. I remember one time that my wife and I took a break to sit on a park bench outside a hardware store. Sitting there, I remember thinking that it sure would be fun to live in Berne. The young man in the cartoon is playing an alphorn, a wooden instrument traditionally used in the Swiss Alps for intercommunication and seasonal festivals. More commonly today, it is used as a musical instrument.

"I *said* Berne Swiss Days are not for a few months, so let's cool it on the alphorn practice for a while."

THE THREE RIVERS

This last cartoon leaves us with the biggest reason that Fort Wayne, Indiana, exists in the first place. It's because of the confluence of the Saint Joseph, Saint Marys and Maumee rivers in the middle of downtown. This area has been a significant home to various Indigenous cultures for ten thousand years because of the river access, fertile soil, and abundant wildlife. Around 1712, the Miami people settled here, calling it Kekionga, which meant "blackberry bush." Later, the French, British, and American settlers came here to use the rivers as a mode of transportation for the fur trade, among other pursuits. Now days, the focus seems to be on the revitalization of the rivers as a link to our past and a look to the future. Because of the city's riverfront development project, our three rivers are gaining prominence, becoming more fun, and helping to further solidify the identity of our hometown, Fort Wayne, Indiana.

"Yes, the rivers in Fort Wayne are great. But, honestly, this is more about avoiding summer road construction."

ABOUT THE OTTER

The otter is a furry aquatic mammal that...Wait!

Oh, I'm sorry! I guess they said *Author*, not Otter. Well, moving on.

My name is Steve Smeltzer, and I am not an otter. However, I am a human and I grew up (but never really matured) in Fort Wayne, Indiana. Our loving family of four included my mom, Ruth, who was always dreaming up a new idea; my dad, Homer, who was a brilliant commercial artist/cartoonist; and my sister, Becky, who was a school teacher for years and is now a prolific writer and author of four books in the *Marigold and the Marvelous Misfits* series.

I started drawing early and was the first male child in our family to have my artwork featured on the prestigious Smeltzer refrigerator.

I was pretty much resting on my laurels until that fateful day in second grade when my best friend since first grade, Jeff Stone, drew an epic rendition of an image from the book *Mike Mulligan and His Steam Shovel*. Our teacher, Miss Havens, made such a big deal about it that I thought she would start proceedings to have it included in an exhibit at the Louvre Museum in Paris. It was the kick in the pants I needed to jump-start my interest in drawing.

When I was 11, I retired from my "art career" to take drum lessons and made music my priority. Eventually, I started teaching drums and currently, I play drums for a few bands in the area, and I teach drums at Sweetwater Academy of Music and Technology three days a week. On the other days of the week, I draw cartoons for magazines, including *Chicago Health*, *Wall Street Journal*, and *Reader's Digest*. For years, I drew cartoons for *Fort Wayne Magazine*, where the cartoons in this book first appeared.

Sometimes, people ask where I get ideas for cartoons, and I often tell them the same thing: coffee.

However, the most important aspect of writing cartoons for me came from my elementary school days. I would walk about one block home to eat with my dad, who took his lunch hour to come home and fix my lunch. We'd sit in front of the TV and watch soap operas while inserting alternative dialog in the actors' lines. I think that trained me to look for funny options in everyday life.

Thanks for taking a look at my first-ever book. And watch out, I may be studying you for my next cartoon! :)

If you enjoyed my cartoons, you can find more of my work at https://www.smeltzercartoons.com/

Also, check out *Fort Wayne in a Nutshell* book on Facebook
www.facebook.com/profile.php?id=61561919542484

Made in the USA
Middletown, DE
10 December 2024

66637977R00049